Instant Pot Whole 30 Cookbook

Quick and Easy
Instant Pot Whole 30
Recipes for Your Family

James Houck

Copyright © 2018 James Houck
All rights reserved.

TABLE OF CONTENTS

1	What is the Concept of Whole 30 and the Whole 30 Challenge?	Pg. 4
2	30 Advantages of Whole 30 Foods	Pg. 6
3	What to Avoid While on the Whole 30 Challenge?	Pg. 10
4	Side Effects to Know About	Pg. 11
5	Instant Pot Whole 30 Chicken Recipes	Pg. 12
6	Instant Pot Whole 30 Seafood Recipes	Pg. 30
7	Instant Pot Whole 30 Pork Recipes	Pg. 42
8	Instant Pot Whole 30 Beef Recipes	Pg. 65
9	About the Author	Pg. 79

COPYRIGHT 2018 BY JAMES HOUCK - ALL RIGHTS RESERVED.

This document is geared towards providing exact and reliable information in regard to the topic and issue covered. The publication is sold on the idea that the publisher is not required to render an accounting, officially permitted, or otherwise, qualified services. If advice is necessary, legal or professional, a practiced individual in the profession should be ordered.

From a Declaration of Principles which was accepted and approved equally by a Committee of the American Bar Association and a Committee of Publishers and Associations.

In no way is it legal to reproduce, duplicate, or transmit any part of this document by either electronic means or in printed format. Recording of this publication is strictly prohibited and any storage of this document is not allowed unless with written permission from the publisher. All rights reserved.

The information provided herein is stated to be truthful and consistent, in that any liability, in terms of inattention or otherwise, by any usage or abuse of any policies, processes, or directions contained within is the solitary and utter responsibility of the recipient reader. Under no circumstances will any legal responsibility or blame be held against the publisher for any reparation, damages, or monetary loss due to the information herein, either directly or indirectly.

Respective authors own all copyrights not held by the publisher. The information herein is offered for informational purposes solely and is universal as so. The presentation of the information is without a contract or any type of guarantee assurance.

The trademark, Whole 30, is used without any consent, and the publication of the trademark is without permission or backing by the trademark owner. All trademarks and brands within this book are for clarifying purposes only and are the owned by the owners themselves, not affiliated with this document.

WHAT IS THE CONCEPT OF WHOLE 30 AND THE WHOLE 30 CHALLENGE?

A Whole 30 diet refers to the 30-day marked diet that focuses on intake of whole food and elimination of alcohol, sugar, legumes, grains, dairy and soy from the meals. The Whole 30 diet is designed to put a restriction on unnecessary and irregular consumption of these items. The main aim of the program is to bring down the weight and stress levels by extracting energy from the right sources.

The list of food groups one is allowed to consume are:
- Vegetables

    Vegetables are an integral part of Whole 30 plan. The vegetables are low in calories and contain all types of nutrients. Consumption of vegetables also reduces the risk of diseases like diabetes and heart diseases. One must aim at including lots of vegetables in every meal. Green vegetables work the best.
- Fruits

    One of the most common myths is that fruits contain hidden sugar which might affect one's diet. But here is the myth buster tip: Fruits contain natural sugar which is full of vitamins, fibers, and minerals. Fruits are included in the diet to bridge the gap of your sweet cravings. One must aim at consuming about 2 cups of fruits every day.
- Fats

    Fats don't increase your weight or make you fat! Fats, in turn, help you to absorb fat-soluble nutrients. They also keep you full that means, you will not feel hungry every now and then and your heart will be healthy too. Oils one must include in their plan are avocado oil, olive oil, coconut oil and canola oil. Other sources of healthy fats include olives, nuts, and avocado. One must avoid packaged food and items made up of hydrogenated oils in this diet program.
- Proteins

    Another important nutrient is protein that helps you build muscles, keep the skin clean and hairs shinier and healthy. One can find ample source of protein in eggs, yogurt nuts, meat, and seafood. One must aim at consuming proteins through whole meal foods only and should avoid sauces, protein shakes and bars.

The diet goes on for 30 days where participants have to abide by certain rules. They are advised not to measure their weight or calories in meanwhile. Once the diet program is completed, they are counseled to draw a personal list of food items, another list stating the health consequences as well as other useful information about the changes felt. The diet program has helped in curing various lifestyle-related conditions and diseases.

The diet has been distributed in certain phases which are mentioned as follows:

- STEP 1: SELECTING THE START DATE

    Planning plays an important role in the 30-day diet. Select a suitable start date while keeping every aspect in mind. Make sure to avoid any big, important or personal events or festivals in the month you are planning to perform this challenge. However, there is no one fixed date to perform the program, thus, whenever to decide to perform the challenge, make sure you perform it well without skipping a day.

- STEP 2: IMPOSING RESTRICTIONS

    This diet helps you awaken both mentally and physically. To achieve success in this program, one needs to impose certain restrictions and abide by the rules. The participant will have to cut down on certain food groups, replace the sources of energy and have a firm control over one's cravings. The book follows a list of foods to avoid and list of foods to consume on your diet journey.

- STEP 3: BELIEVING IN SELF

    Self-control and firm willpower is the key to success. One should believe that this diet is not hard and you can make through it. One should commit that they won't cheat their meals and will stick to the rules. The last but not the least, you can do this, you will do this!

- STEP 4: HIDING THE SCALES

    Finally, you must hide the measuring scale. Yes, you read it right. The whole idea of following a Whole 30 diet is to transform into a healthier being, rather than focusing on weight loss like other diets. Though weight loss is one of the advantages of this diet, but still hiding the scales and not checking your weight for following 30 days will make you feel body positive.

Once you have prepared for all the four steps well, you are ready to embark upon the journey of changing your lifestyle with the Whole 30 program.

30 ADVANTAGES OF WHOLE 30 FOODS

- CONSISTENT ENERGY LEVELS: With changes in energy sources, you will notice a consistency in performing activities and working with faster speed than before.

- IMPROVED SLEEP SCHEDULES: With the elimination of sugars and intake of proteins or fats, your sleep will be for sound, longer and profound.

- BIDDING GOODBYE TO DIGESTIVE ISSUES: Digestive issues like indigestion, stomach aches etc. will take a back seat as the body will adapt to intake of more vegetables in this program.

- OPTIMISTIC APPROACH: You will feel better as the program will approach the end, waking up to more optimistic ideas every day.

- SWITCHING TO HEALTHIER OPTIONS: To boost in the fit lifestyle, the diet will include intake of a lot of vegetables. This will lead to better nutrition and healthier living.

- INCREASED WATER INTAKE: Since all the other drinks are restricted to this diet, your body's requirements will be met by water, which in turn will act as great measure.

- BEING HAPPY: With stability in blood sugar level, you will feel happy from inside. You will feel full and satisfied all day long.

- FOCUS AND DETERMINATION: Since the Whole 30 diet involves improving focus and alertness; you will find yourself more determined and getting clear ideas.

- SAVORING FOOD: Rather than gobbling and eating in excess, you will learn to appreciate the flavor and the nutrition you are gaining from every bite you eat. This will cut down the extra diet, thus, leading to weight loss.

- EMOTIONAL RELATIONSHIP WITH FOOD: With help of insulin management, the body will pass better signals about real hunger and appetite. This will help in avoiding unnecessary meals from day to day life. It will curb and remove the emotional attachment with food.

- PEACE OF MIND: The enhanced state of mind will help to remove anxiety and overthinking habits, thus, providing a calmness and peace to the brain. Since you will be happy, you will ultimately achieve the peace of mind too.

- EXPERIMENTING AND INVENTING: When you will indulge yourself in the Whole 30 plan, you will find yourself in the kitchen, experimenting with several ingredients and inventing your own personal dishes!

- NEW FAVORITES: With so many recipes to have around and by restricting the consumption of beans, grains, and dairy, you might notice a change in your taste or favorite dishes as well.

- KNOWING YOURSELF BETTER: By focusing on your body's demands and requirements for next 30 days, you will learn about your favorites, your dislikes, self-care, triggers, hunger periods etc.

- ORGANIZED LIFESTYLE: The most important concept behind the Whole 30 program is to organize your eating habits, leading to being better and organized in other sectors of life as well.

- MOTIVATION AND WILLPOWER: On this diet, you will find the motivation to continue it for the planned period of 30 days. You will feel the willpower rising within yourself with raised hormonal response and self-control over activities.

- INCREASED FERTILITY: Cutting down sugar will cut down the inflammation which is one of the biggest factors in lowering down the fertility in females. Thus, following this diet will be beneficial for the females who wish to increase their fertility rate naturally.

- CONTROLLING SUGAR: You will have a firm control over sugar intake and you will be able to curb your sugar demands after the end of the program, making a big difference.

- JOINT PAIN RELIEF: Removal of inflammation-causing foods reduces the inflammation around cushion pads of the knees, curing the issue of joint pain. Joint pain relief is usually experienced in adults, and following the whole 30 program will cure it.

- BALANCED HORMONES: With the right nutrients, your body will heal gradually, where you will experience lesser cravings and mood swings. You will be able to manage your insulin levels and glucose levels.

- CLEARER SKIN: Younger looking skin is just a diet away. You will feel a smooth and beautiful change in your skin with a natural glow after this program.

- LOSING WEIGHT: If the ultimate aim is losing weight, you can accomplish it with right types of meals. You might even develop some muscles with help of exercise.

- PRACTICAL NOTION OF FOOD: Food will not be the ultimate focus of your life; you will be able to look at the practical notion of it for developing a better version of yourself.

- ENHANCED WORKOUTS: Working out with consumption of right kind of food is nothing less than bliss to a healthy and fit life. Intake of fruits and vegetables along with the right type of exercise for your body will bring a major positive change in your life.

- MANAGING AND REMOVING DISEASES: The Whole 30 diet will reverse the symptoms of some diseases and cure other illnesses like asthma, diabetes etc. It also helps to fix and cure chronic diseases.

- SAYING NO TO BLOATING: As soon as the legumes and dairy products are gone, say bye to bloating too. Welcome flatter tummy!

- SHINIER HAIR, STRONGER NAILS: With enriched diet and right nutrients, you will get glossier and shinier hair. The problem of chipped nails will be solved with the growth of stronger nails.

- REDUCED OBSESSIONS ABOUT BEING OVERWEIGHT: Since one of the rules of the diet is that you cannot measure your weight, you will be focused on improving your way of leaving than losing weight or worrying about being overweight.

- INFLUENCING OTHERS: By sticking to the program schedule, not only you will develop an optimistic approach yourself, but also, you will be able to positively influence others preaching healthy lifestyle.

- ACCEPTANCE: By the end of the diet, you will able to accept the fact about your body, its image and will learn to love, care and celebrate the idea of being physically and mentally fit.

WHAT TO AVOID WHILE ON THE WHOLE 30 CHALLENGE?

While on a 30-day diet challenge, some foods are absolutely restricted. These food items are a complete no-no and are mentioned as follows:

- DAIRY

  Dairy products like cow milk, cheese, cream, yogurt, sour cream, and butter cannot be consumed while you are on a whole 30 challenge. However, there is an exception to the dairy rule that ghee can be consumed.

- ALCOHOL

  Alcohol cannot be used for drinking or cooking purposes while you choose the Whole 30 diet. This also means that you cannot intake any added flavors like vanilla extract etc.

- GRAINS

  Absolutely no rice, corn, quinoa, rye, wheat, sorghum, millet, buckwheat, amaranth, sprouted grains or bulgur for next 30 days!

- LEGUMES

  Another restricted component is legumes, meaning no beans, soy, tofu, miso, peas, chickpeas, peanuts or lentils for following 30 days. Cutting down legumes also helps to balance lots of issues well.

- JUNK

  Junk means something that you do not have to eat on this diet. No pizzas, pancakes, burgers etc. Try to emotionally cut off yourself from having junk to ensure success in this diet program.

- SULFITES AND MSG

  The participant should totally avoid consuming any type of processed food. Check the labels and avoid any items which include MSG, carrageenan or sulfites in it.

- SUGAR

  Sugar is present in various forms in various items. Cut down everything. Ignore any real or artificial intake in form of syrups, honey, stevia, agave etc. Check the label on everything and use items with no or minimal sugar level in them.

SIDE EFFECTS TO KNOW ABOUT

Whole 30 is not just a weight loss program, it is more of lifestyle treatment plan. With all the benefits involved, the diet comes up with side effects of its own which can sometimes weaken your willpower and motivation to continue the challenge. If you are looking to pick up this challenge, have a look at the list of side effects as well which you might experience in one of the thirty days.

- HUNGER
  Being new to any diet program is always hard. And one of the hardest things to do is curbing your hunger. Sudden outbreaks, cravings etc. will make you eat your favorite thing, which is restricted in the diet. That is why self-control is really important in this challenge.

- EUPHORIA
  While eating vegetables and organics, you will feel light headed and happy in the beginning. You will be able to see changes and become happy quickly. This is euphoria and it doesn't last long. After a short period of time, everything will subside and things will get back to reality.

- MOOD SWINGS
  Mood swings will take over you as soon as you choose the program and restrict yourself to consume some food items. In the initial days, you will feel cranky and irritated, which is quite normal. Don't worry, just take a bath or a massage and do things that make you calm and happy.

- DULLNESS AND SLUGGISHNESS
  You will notice a constant light headache, achy joints, and painful body. Due to the restriction of carbs, you will feel low throughout the day. As the body will adapt to the refined energy source, it will slowly fade away sluggishness.

- GUILT
  Since the Whole 30 diet is really restrictive in nature, the participant might feel like cheating. Once they cheat, they are not able to come up off the guilt, which continues as a heavy side effect.

- STOMACH ISSUES
  Excess intake of anything is harmful. Since you suddenly switch to intake of excess vegetables, the level of fiber content in your body shoots up. Fiber may add to discomfort as it might lead to constipation or diarrhea. You might also experience stomach aches and bowels.

INSTANT POT WHOLE 30 CHICKEN RECIPES

CREAMY SOUTHWEST CHICKEN

SERVING SIZE: 1 SERVING
SERVINGS PER RECIPE: 5
CALORIES: 291 PER SERVING
PREPARATION TIME: 10 MINUTES
COOKING TIME: 15 MINUTES

INGREDIENTS:

- Chicken thighs/breasts- 1.5 lbs., boneless
- Coconut cream/ coconut milk- ½ cup
- Red bell peppers- 2, sliced
- Chicken broth- 1 cup
- Paprika- 2 teaspoons
- Chili powder- 1 tablespoon
- Ground coriander- 1 teaspoon
- Ground cumin- 1 teaspoon
- Garlic powder0 1 teaspoon
- Cayenne pepper- ½ teaspoon
- Sea salt- 1 teaspoon
- Water- 1 tablespoon
- Lime juice- ¼ cup
- Arrowroot- 1 tablespoon
- Salt and pepper- as per taste
- Cilantro- for garnishing

NUTRITION INFORMATION:

- Total fat: 2.9 g
- Carbohydrate: 32.4 g
- Fiber: 7.1 g
- Sugar: 0 g
- Protein: 36.1 g

DIRECTIONS:

1. Heat the pot first by selecting the sauté function on the Instant Pot.

2. Take a small bowl and mix all the spices in it. Once this spice mixture is ready, use it to rub over the chicken and coat it properly.

3. Brush the bottom of the pot with oil so the chicken doesn't stick to it. Place the coated chicken it. Now, cook the chicken for 2 minutes on each side to secure the flavor of spices in it. Once done, select Cancel.

4. Add leftover ingredients i.e. lime juice, chicken broth, peppers and leftover spices in the pot. Stir well and seal the lid.

5. Cook the chicken on high pressure by selecting manual, for next 7 minutes. Let the steam get out after the cooking is complete.

6. Open the lid and add coconut milk or coconut cream to it. Pour in water and mix well to form sauce-like consistency. You can thicken the sauce using arrowroot.

7. Add salt and pepper as per taste.

8. Garnish the creamy chicken with cilantro and serve it with rice, pasta or noodles.

DELICIOUS CHICKEN TACOS

SERVING SIZE: 1 SERVING
SERVINGS PER RECIPE: 4
CALORIES: 140 PER SERVING
PREPARATION TIME: 10 MINUTES
COOKING TIME: 25 MINUTES

INGREDIENTS:

- Chicken thighs/breasts- 1 lb., boneless
- Salsa- ½ cup
- Water- ¼ cup
- Garlic powder- ½ teaspoon
- Ground cumin- 1 teaspoon
- Chili powder- 1 teaspoon
- Cayenne pepper- 1/8 teaspoon
- Ground coriander- ½ teaspoon
- Black pepper- ¼ teaspoon
- Sea salt- ¼ teaspoon
- Cilantro- chopped
- Salad greens/ wraps
- For topping: Olives, lime wedge or avocado

NUTRITION INFORMATION:

- Total fat: 3 g
- Carbohydrate: 4 g
- Fiber: 0 g
- Sugar: 1 g
- Protein: 26 g

DIRECTIONS:

1. In the bottom of Instant Pot, place all the ingredients properly except the salad greens. Seal the pot's lid in place.

2. Press the 'Poultry' button and adjust the cooking timer to 17-19 minutes. The cooking time depends upon the thickness of the chicken breasts.

3. When the chicken is cooked, allow the steam to release for next 10 minutes.

4. Remove the lid and with the help of a fork, shred the chicken in the pot itself. If there is excess water still left, set the pot at 'sauté' setting to cook for another 8 minutes.

5. Your chicken filling is done! Serve it in a wrap or with salad greens, garnished with fresh cilantro, and with your favorite topping. Make sure the topping doesn't involve any packaged item or added sugar.

CHICKEN AND SWEET POTATO CURRY

SERVING SIZE: 1 SERVING
SERVINGS PER RECIPE: 4
CALORIES: 325 PER SERVING
PREPARATION TIME: 15 MINUTES
COOKING TIME: 20 MINUTES

INGREDIENTS:

- Chicken breast- 1 lb., boneless, cubed
- Sweet potato- 2 cups, cubes
- Green beans- 2 cups, trimmed
- Yellow onion- ½, medium size, diced
- Garlic cloves- 3, minced
- Red pepper- 1, sliced
- Cumin- 1 teaspoon
- Curry powder- 3 tablespoons
- Ground turmeric- 1 teaspoon
- Sea salt- ½ teaspoon
- Cayenne- ½ teaspoon
- Chicken broth- 2/3 cup
- Coconut oil- 2 teaspoons
- Coconut milk- 1 can
- Serve with cilantro, cashews and cauliflower rice

NUTRITION INFORMATION:

- Total fat: 15 g
- Carbohydrate: 19 g
- Fiber: 4 g
- Sugar: 6 g
- Protein: 26 g

DIRECTIONS:

1. Set the setting of the Instant Pot to 'sauté'. In the bottom of the pot, add onion, ghee, and garlic. Sauté the ingredients until the onions become pink and translucent.

2. Now, set the setting to manual and set the temperature to high. Add sweet potatoes, chicken, green beans, red pepper, curry, broth, turmeric, cumin, sea salt, and cayenne. Seal the lid of the Instant Pot. Set the timer for 12 minutes.

3. Once the timer beeps, release the steam. Once the pressure is released, again select the sauté setting. Add coconut milk and cook for another 2-3 minutes. If you want the consistency thicker, you can a tablespoon of arrowroot to it.

4. Take a skillet and sauté cauliflower rice in it with 1 teaspoon of ghee over medium heat.

5. Serve the sweet potato and chicken curry over cauliflower rice garnished with freshly chopped cilantro and cashews.

CHICKEN TIKKA MASALA

SERVING SIZE: 1 CUP
SERVINGS PER RECIPE: 4
CALORIES: 460 PER SERVING
PREPARATION TIME: 10 MINUTES
COOKING TIME: 20 MINUTES

INGREDIENTS:

- Chicken breast- 1.5 lbs., boneless, skinless
- Onion- 1, small size, chopped
- Ginger- 1, peeled, chopped
- Garlic cloves- 3, minced
- Tomatoes- 1, diced
- Chicken broth- ½ cup
- Lemon juice- 1 lemon
- Olive oil- 2 tablespoons
- Garam masala- 1 teaspoon
- Paprika- 2 teaspoons
- Ground coriander- 1 teaspoon
- Ground turmeric- 1 teaspoon
- Cumin- 2 teaspoons
- Cayenne pepper- 1/4 teaspoon
- Coconut milk- ½ cup
- Cilantro/Basil- chopped, for garnishing

NUTRITION INFORMATION:

- Total fat: 27 g
- Carbohydrate: 19 g
- Fiber: 0 g
- Sugar: 0 g
- Protein: 32 g

DIRECTIONS:

1. Choose the setting of the Instant Pot as 'sauté'. Add ginger, olive oil, garlic and onion once the pot is hot. Cook the ingredients for 3-4 minutes, while stirring occasionally.

2. Once done, add the remaining spices to the cooked mixture. Add tomatoes to form a puree-like mixture and stir well. Place the chicken breasts on top of the sauce and pour chicken broth over it. Seal the lid and cook for 7 minutes at high pressure on the manual setting.

3. Use quick release option to release the excess steam. Shred the chicken into pieces in the pot itself.

4. Again select the sauté setting and simmer the chicken for 5 minutes. Pour in coconut milk and lemon juice. Add salt if desired.

5. Serve the chicken tikka masala with rice or flatbread, garnished with fresh cilantro or basil. Serve the chicken tikka masala hot for best flavors.

CHICKEN CACCIATORE

SERVING SIZE: 1 SERVING
SERVINGS PER RECIPE: 4-6
CALORIES: 128 PER SERVING
PREPARATION TIME: 10 MINUTES
COOKING TIME: 15 MINUTES

INGREDIENTS:

- Chicken breasts/chicken thighs- 2 lbs.
- Onion- 1, medium size, chopped
- Tomatoes- 1, diced
- Mushrooms- 8 oz., sliced
- Garlic cloves- 3, minced
- Green bell pepper- 1, large size, chopped
- Olive oil- 2 tablespoons
- Red wine vinegar- ¼ cup
- Tomato paste- 3 tablespoons
- Chicken broth- ¾ cup
- Dried oregano- 1 teaspoon
- Dried rosemary- 1 teaspoon
- Paprika- 1 teaspoon
- Dried thyme- 1 teaspoon
- Salt- 1 teaspoon
- Fresh thyme/basil- 2 tablespoons, for serving
- Salt and pepper- as per taste

NUTRITION INFORMATION:

- Total fat: 3 g
- Carbohydrate: 4 g
- Fiber: 0 g
- Sugar: 0 g
- Protein: 21 g

DIRECTIONS:

1. To heat up the pot, select the sauté function in the Instant Pot.

2. While the pot heats up, season the chicken with salt and pepper. Brush the bottom of the Instant Pot with oil and place chicken in it. Cook the chicken for 1-2 minutes on both the sides. Once the chicken gets cooked completely, remove it aside and sauté onions in the pot for next 2 minutes. Now, add garlic and cook for next 1 minute.

3. Take a bowl and add all the dry spices to it that is, paprika, oregano, thyme, rosemary, and salt. Add tomato paste, spice mixture, tomatoes and vinegar to the onion and garlic mixture in the pot. Stir and combine everything properly.

4. Using this sauce, coat the chicken and add remaining vegetables like bell pepper and mushrooms to the pot. Pour chicken broth on top of marinated chicken. Seal the lid.

5. Select the manual settings and cook the dish for next 8 minutes at high pressure.

6. Release the steam and open the lid. Stir the contents well and allow the sauce to thicken. Add salt and pepper as per taste.

7. Serve your delicious chicken cacciatore with potatoes, noodles and garnish with basil and thyme. Make sure the noodles you are using are whole wheat in nature.

CHICKEN ZUCCHINI NOODLE SOUP

SERVING SIZE: 1 CUP
SERVINGS PER RECIPE: 6-8
CALORIES: 104 PER SERVING
PREPARATION TIME: 10 MINUTES
COOKING TIME: 8 MINUTES

INGREDIENTS:

- Chicken breasts- 1.5 lbs.
- Celery- 3 stalks, chopped
- Onion- 1, small size, diced
- Carrots- 1 cup, chopped
- Zucchini- 2, medium size
- Chicken broth- 64 oz.
- Fresh thyme- 1 tablespoon, chopped
- Fresh rosemary- 1 tablespoon, chopped
- Apple cider vinegar- ¼ cup
- Dried basil- 2 teaspoon
- Bay leaf- 1
- Dried dill- 1 teaspoon
- Lemon pepper- 2 teaspoons
- Sea salt- 1 teaspoon

NUTRITION INFORMATION:

- Total fat: 3 g
- Carbohydrate: 4 g
- Fiber: 1 g
- Sugar: 3 g
- Protein: 12 g

DIRECTIONS:

1. Place the chicken in the bottom of the Instant Pot along with all the vegetables except zucchini. Pour in apple cider vinegar and chicken broth.

2. Add all the herbs and seal the lid of the pot. Cook the chicken for about 10 minutes at high pressure to soften the chicken and to mix the flavors well

3. Once the chicken is done, shred it using a fork. Release the pressure and once the venting is complete, remove the pot's lid and add zucchini noodles to the soup.

4. Serve hot, seasoned with salt and pepper. Garnish with extra zucchini as per requirements.

HARISSA CHICKEN

SERVING SIZE: 1 SERVING
SERVINGS PER RECIPE: 4-6
CALORIES: 206 PER SERVING
PREPARATION TIME: 12 MINUTES
COOKING TIME: 12 MINUTES

INGREDIENTS:

- Chicken breasts- 1.5 lbs.
- Red peppers- 12 oz., roasted
- Adobo sauce- 2 teaspoons
- Chipotle peppers- 2
- Olive oil- 1 tablespoon
- Apple cider vinegar- 1 tablespoon
- Ground coriander- 1 teaspoon
- Ground cumin- 1 teaspoon
- Lemon juice of ½ lemon
- Caraway seeds- ½ teaspoon
- Salt- 1 teaspoon
- Garlic cloves- 4, minced
- Onion- ½ cup, diced
- Cilantro- 3 tablespoons
- Salt and pepper- as per taste

NUTRITION INFORMATION:

- Total fat: 8 g
- Carbohydrate: 1 g
- Fiber: 1 g
- Sugar: 1 g
- Protein: 32 g

DIRECTIONS:

1. Start by preparing the sauce for your recipe. Using a food processor, blend chipotle peppers, red peppers, spices, herbs, lemon, vinegar, and garlic. Add oil and blend until everything smoothens out.

2. Choose the sauté setting in your pot. Heat it up and brush the bottom of the pot with olive oil. Sauté the diced onions in it.

3. Place the chicken in the bottom and topple it with blended sauce. Lock the lid of the pot and cook at high pressure for 7 minutes at manual setting.

4. Use quick release. Shred the chicken inside the pot using a fork.

5. Serve your Harissa chicken warm and garnish with cilantro.

CHICKEN AND KALE SOUP

SERVING SIZE: 4 OZ
SERVINGS PER RECIPE: 4
CALORIES: 123 PER SERVING
PREPARATION TIME: 5 MINUTES
COOKING TIME: 15 MINUTES

INGREDIENTS:

- Shredded chicken breast- 1 lb.
- Carrot- 3, peeled, chopped
- Onion- 1, medium size, chopped
- Celery- 4 stalks, chopped
- Bay leaves- 3
- Olive oil- 2 tablespoons
- Black pepper- ½ teaspoon
- Dried oregano- ¼ teaspoon
- Dried thyme- ½ teaspoon
- Salt- 1 teaspoon
- Chicken broth- 4 cups
- Fish sauce- ½ teaspoon
- Kale- 1, large size, chopped

NUTRITION INFORMATION:

- Total fat: 4 g
- Carbohydrate: 10 g
- Fiber: 0 g
- Sugar: 0 g
- Protein: 13 g

DIRECTIONS:

1. Select the sauté setting on Instant Pot. Add onion and olive oil to the pot and sauté till the onions become tender, for like 5 minutes.

2. Now, add celery, carrots, salt, bay leaves, thyme, pepper and oregano to the pot. Sauté until everything has completely mixed for next 1 minute.

3. Pour in the chicken broth. Cover the pot with lid and select the cancel button to cancel the sauté function. Now, press the soup function and adjust the timer to 4 minutes at high pressure. Once the main cooking is done, depressurize the cooker and allow the steam to release through valves.

4. Remove the lid and add the kale and chicken to the pot. Let the soup rest for a minute or two. Ensure that the kale has turned green. Add salt and pepper as per taste, and fish sauce before serving.

BUTTER CHICKEN

SERVING SIZE: 1 SERVING (8 OUNCES)
SERVINGS PER RECIPE: 4
CALORIES: 270 PER SERVING
PREPARATION TIME: 15 MINUTES
COOKING TIME: 17 MINUTES

INGREDIENTS:

- Chicken thighs- 2-3 lbs., boneless, skinless
- Onion- 1 ½, large size, chopped
- Garlic powder- 2 teaspoons
- Ginger powder- 2 teaspoons
- Salt- 2 ½ teaspoons
- Paprika- 2 teaspoons
- Turmeric- 2 teaspoons
- Cayenne powder- 1 ½ teaspoons
- Garam masala- 2 teaspoons
- Tomato paste- 2 cups
- Tomatoes- 1-2 cups
- Coconut milk- 2 cups
- Cilantro- ½ cup
- Almond- ½ cup

NUTRITION INFORMATION:

- Total fat: 8 g
- Carbohydrate: 33 g
- Fiber: 2 g
- Sugar: 2 g
- Protein: 18 g

DIRECTIONS:

1. Select the sauté setting on Instant Pot and melt the ghee in it. Add onions and salt to it to sauté. Cook until the onions become translucent. While the onions cook for 2-3 minutes, cover the pot with lid.

2. Now, add ginger, garlic, paprika, and turmeric and cayenne powder to the pot. Stir well until a fragrant spice mixture is received.

3. Once the spice mixture is ready, add coconut milk and canned tomatoes to the pot. Scrap off the spices stuck at the bottom. Add chicken to the pot and mix.

4. Now, cook the chicken at high pressure for 8-10 minutes. Make sure the setting is in manual mode.

5. Release the steam naturally while the chicken settles in the pot. Pour in coconut cream, tomato paste cilantro, and garam masala. Add more salt as per taste.

6. Garnish the mouthwatering butter chicken with chopped almonds and cilantro.

7. Serve hot for a satisfying and a complete healthy meal.

INSTANT POT WHOLE 30 SEAFOOD RECIPES

LEMON PEPPER SALMON

SERVING SIZE: 4 OZ
SERVINGS PER RECIPE: 3-4
CALORIES: 239 PER SERVING
PREPARATION TIME: 5 MINUTES
COOKING TIME: 10 MINUTES

INGREDIENTS:

- Salmon fillet- 1 pound, skin on
- Water- ¾ cup
- Lemon- ½, sliced
- Zucchini- 1
- Red bell pepper- 1, chopped
- Carrot- 1, chopped
- Ghee- 3 teaspoons
- Salt- ¼ teaspoon
- Pepper- ¼ teaspoon
- Sprigs of dill, parsley, basil

NUTRITION INFORMATION:

- Total fat: 17 g
- Carbohydrate: 1 g
- Fiber: 0 g
- Sugar: 0 g
- Protein: 20 g

DIRECTIONS:

1. Add water to the Instant Pot and mix all the herbs in it. Place the Instant Pot on the steamer rack. Place the salmon the rack. Make sure the fillet's skin is down.

2. Brush the salmon fillet with a mixture of ghee, pepper, and salt. Cover it using the lemon slices.

3. Lock the lid of Instant Pot and use the steam function to cook the fillet for next 3 minutes.

4. As the timer beeps, release the pressure; remove the lid and remove the salmon from the rack. Place it on the plate.

5. Remove the excess herbs and add vegetables to the pot. Sauté those in the pot for further 2-3 minutes.

6. Serve the freshly cooked vegetables with salmon with the sauce.

BOILED SHRIMPS

SERVING SIZE: 6 OZ
SERVINGS PER RECIPE: 5
CALORIES: 182 PER SERVING
PREPARATION TIME: 3 MINUTES
COOKING TIME: 12 MINUTES

INGREDIENTS:

- Shrimp- 1.5 lbs.
- Potatoes- 1 lb.
- Sausage- 1, smoked
- Mushrooms- 1 pack
- Seasoning- 2 tablespoons
- Garlic- 1 tablespoon, minced
- Garlic powder- ½ tablespoon
- Salt- ½ tablespoon
- Onion powder- ½ tablespoon
- Pepper- 1 tablespoon
- Chicken broth
- Water

NUTRITION INFORMATION:

- Total fat: 2 g
- Carbohydrate: 5 g
- Fiber: 0 g
- Sugar: 0 g
- Protein: 31 g

DIRECTIONS:

1. Cut the white potatoes into cubes and add it to the Instant Pot. Pour in chicken broth, salt and 1 tablespoon of seasoning. Cover the Instant Pot with the lid and cook for next 3 minutes on beans setting at high pressure.

2. Meanwhile, chop the sausage into slices and remove the stems from the mushrooms.

3. Once the potatoes are done, release the pressure and add mushrooms, sausage, shrimp and rest of the ingredients. Pour in 1 cup of water and keep on stirring to mix everything well.

4. Seal the lid and cook the contents for another 4 minutes at high pressure by selecting the setting for beans.

5. Release the steam again and serve the boiled shrimps hot!

CHINESE STYLE FISH STEAMED WITH GINGER AND SCALLIONS

SERVING SIZE: 1 PORTION
SERVINGS PER RECIPE: 4
CALORIES: 171 PER SERVING
PREPARATION TIME: 10 MINUTES
COOKING TIME: 10 MINUTES

INGREDIENTS:

- Whitefish (Tilapia)- 1 pound
- Peanut oil- 1 tablespoon
- Soy sauce- 3 tablespoons
- Chinese black bean paste- 1 tablespoon
- Rice wine- 2 tablespoons
- Garlic- 1 teaspoon
- Ginger- 1 teaspoon, minced
- Ginger- 2 tablespoons, julienned
- Scallions- ¼ cup, julienned
- Cilantro- ¼ cup, chopped

NUTRITION INFORMATION:

- Total fat: 5 g
- Carbohydrate: 4 g
- Fiber: 1 g
- Sugar: 1 g
- Protein: 24 g

DIRECTIONS:

1. Cut the fish into pieces and lay it on a plate. Mix soy sauce, garlic, Chinese black bean paste, rice wine and minced ginger in a bowl to form a sauce.

2. Pour the freshly prepared sauce over the fish pieces. Allow it to marinate for next 20-30 minutes. Keep the excess marinade aside for further use.

3. Chop all the vegetables and keep them aside.

4. Pour 2 cups of water in Instant Pot and place the steamer in it.

5. Place the marinated fish in the steamer basket.

6. Cook the fish at low pressure for 2 minutes. Release the steam immediately.

7. Take a separate saucepan and add oil to it. Once the oil heats up, add ginger, scallions, and cilantro to it. Sauté it well for 2 minutes and add the leftover marinade. Let the contents boil until cooked enough.

8. Pour this boiled marinade over the fish and serve fresh.

SEAFOOD GUMBO

SERVING SIZE: 1 CUP
SERVINGS PER RECIPE: 8
CALORIES: 156 PER SERVING
PREPARATION TIME: 10 MINUTES
COOKING TIME: 12 MINUTES

INGREDIENTS:

- Sea bass fillets- 24 ounces
- Celery ribs- 4, diced
- Shrimp- 2 pounds, raw
- Ghee- 3 tablespoons
- Yellow onions- 2, diced
- Tomatoes- 28 ounces, diced
- Bell peppers- 2, diced
- Cajun seasoning- 3 tablespoons
- Bay leaves- 3
- Tomato paste- ¼ cup
- Broth- 1 ½ cups
- Sea salt and black pepper- as per taste

NUTRITION INFORMATION:

- Total fat: 5 g
- Carbohydrate: 9 g
- Fiber: 2 g
- Sugar: 0 g
- Protein: 11 g

DIRECTIONS:

1. Season the sea bass fillets properly with sea salt and black pepper. Make sure that the fillets are coated evenly. Sprinkle Cajun seasoning all over it. Keep it aside.

2. Add ghee to the Instant Pot and use the sauté function. As soon as the ghee heats up, add the fillets. Sauté the fillets in ghee for next 4 minutes, cooking on each side. Transfer the fish to the plate once done.

3. Add onions, celery, Cajun seasoning and pepper to the pot and sauté again for next 2 minutes. Press the cancel button. Add diced tomatoes, cooked fish, tomato paste, broth, and bay leaves to the pot. Stir well and seal back the lid.

4. Cook the gumbo for 5 minutes on the manual setting.

5. Push the cancel button once the timer beeps. Vent and release the excess pressure.

6. Once the steam is completely released, add shrimps to the pot and cook for additional 3-4 minutes at sauté setting. Season the gumbo with black pepper and sea salt as desired.

7. Serve hot with chives and cauliflower rice.

FISH TACO BOWLS

SERVING SIZE: 1 BOWL
SERVINGS PER RECIPE: 4
CALORIES: 276 PER SERVING
PREPARATION TIME: 3 MINUTES
COOKING TIME: 12 MINUTES

INGREDIENTS:

- Cod fillets- 3
- Green cabbage- ½ cup, grated
- Cilantro- ½ cup, chopped
- Carrot- 1, large size, peeled, grated
- Avocado- 1, medium size, peeled, diced
- Tomatoes- 2, diced
- Mayonnaise- ½ cup
- Juice of ½ lime
- Orange juice- 2 tablespoons
- Ground cumin- 1 teaspoon
- Garlic salt- 1 teaspoon
- Sea salt- ½ teaspoon
- Olive oil- 1 tablespoon
- Lime wedges- 4,
- Water- 1 cup
- Dash of Sriracha

NUTRITION INFORMATION:

- Total fat: 22 g
- Carbohydrate: 9 g
- Fiber: 3 g
- Sugar: 3 g
- Protein: 13 g

DIRECTIONS:

1. Take a large bowl and combine lime juice, cod fillets, orange juice, ground cumin, garlic salt and olive oil in it. Refrigerate the marinated fish for 15 minutes.

2. Turn your Instant Pot on and add 1 cup water to it. Insert the trivet and place steamer basket on top of it. Place the marinated cod in a steamer basket.

3. Pour and add in all the leftover ingredients. Lock the pot's lid and press the manual button. Set the timer for 3 minutes.

4. Once done, quick release the pressure and unlock the lid.

5. Place the slaw in the bowls, add fish filling on top of it and garnish. Serve.

CHILI LIME SAUCE DRIZZLED SALMON

SERVING SIZE: 1 SERVING
SERVINGS PER RECIPE: 2
CALORIES: 400 PER SERVING
PREPARATION TIME: 10 MINUTES
COOKING TIME: 5 MINUTES

INGREDIENTS:

For steaming salmon:
- Salmon fillets- 2
- Water- 1 cup
- Black pepper and sea salt- as per taste

For chili lime sauce:
- Jalapeno- 1, seeded, diced
- Garlic cloves- 2, minced
- Olive oil- 1 tablespoon
- Juice of 1 lemon
- Honey- 1 tablespoon
- Paprika- ½ teaspoon
- Parsley- 1 tablespoon, chopped
- Cumin- 1/2 teaspoon
- Hot water- 1 tablespoon

NUTRITION INFORMATION:

- Total fat: 25 g
- Carbohydrate: 10.5 g
- Fiber: 0.5 g
- Sugar: 9 g
- Protein: 29 g

DIRECTIONS:

1. Take a bowl and combine all the ingredients required for the sauce in it. Mix well. Set the sauce aside.

2. Add water to the Instant Pot. Insert steam rack and place salmon on it. Season the salmon with black pepper and sea salt.

3. Seal the pot's lid and press the steam setting. Cook the fish at high pressure for 5 minutes. Use the quick release mode to release the pressure and press cancel button.

4. Unlock the lid and place the salmon on the plate. Drizzle the salmon with chili lime sauce.

5. Serve. You can also add lemon wedges for garnishing purpose.

INSTANT POT WHOLE 30 PORK RECIPES

NAPA CABBAGE AND PORK SOUP

SERVING SIZE: 1 CUP
SERVINGS PER RECIPE: 2
CALORIES: 290 PER SERVING
PREPARATION TIME: 10 MINUTES
COOKING TIME: 20 MINUTES

INGREDIENTS:

- Ground pork- 1 pound
- Napa cabbage- 2 pounds
- Onion- 1, small size, diced
- Carrot- 2, peeled and sliced
- Garlic cloves- 2, minced
- Potato- 1, large size, peeled, diced
- Mushrooms- 6, large size, sliced
- Scallions- 3, sliced
- Ghee- 1 teaspoon
- Broth- 6 cups
- Ground black pepper
- Kosher salt

NUTRITION INFORMATION:

- Total fat: 15 g
- Carbohydrate: 12 g
- Fiber: 3 g
- Sugar: 0 g
- Protein: 26 g

DIRECTIONS:

1. Heat ghee in the pot. When the ghee heats up, add onion and salt. Toss well and stir occasionally for 3 minutes.

2. Break the pork into pieces and add it to the pot along with mushrooms and salt. Cook the mushrooms and pork for next 6 minutes. Now add minced garlic and cook for next 30 seconds.

3. Increase the pressure to high and pour the broth. Boil everything.

4. Now, add carrots, potato, and cabbage and boil the soup again.

5. Lock the lid and simmer the soup under high pressure for 5 more minutes. Release the pressure on the manual setting.

6. Season the filling soup with salt and pepper, garnished with scallions.

PORK ROAST IN CAULIFLOWER GRAVY

SERVING SIZE: 1 SERVING
SERVINGS PER RECIPE: 2
CALORIES: 208 PER SERVING
PREPARATION TIME: 10 MINUTES
COOKING TIME: 70 MINUTES

INGREDIENTS:

- Pork roast- 2 to 3 pounds
- Cauliflower- 4 cups, chopped
- Garlic cloves- 4
- Mushrooms- 8 ounces, sliced
- Onion- 1, medium size, chopped
- Celery- 2 ribs
- Sea salt- 1 teaspoon
- Black pepper- ½ teaspoon
- Ghee/Coconut oil- 2 tablespoons
- Water- 2 cups

NUTRITION INFORMATION:

- Total fat: 9 g
- Carbohydrate: 3 g
- Fiber: 0 g
- Sugar: 1 g
- Protein: 26 g

DIRECTIONS:

1. Add onion, cauliflower, celery, garlic, and water at the bottom of the Instant Pot. Place the pork roast on the top and season with pepper and salt as per taste.

2. Cook the contents for 60 minutes under pressure.

3. Release the pressure and remove the pork roast from the pot. Shred it using a fork and place it in a separate dish.

4. Add the cooked vegetables and broth to the blender and blend until smooth.

5. Using the sauté function cook mushrooms with coconut oil for next 3-5 minutes. Add the blended vegetables to the pot and sauté again.

6. Serve the shredded pork well mixed in the cauliflower and mushroom gravy along with whole wheat bread or cauliflower rice.

BABY BACK RIBS

SERVING SIZE: 4 OZ
SERVINGS PER RECIPE: 5
CALORIES: 250 PER SERVING
PREPARATION TIME: 10 MINUTES
COOKING TIME: 40 MINUTES

INGREDIENTS:

Baby back ribs- 3 to 3 ½ lbs.

Chili powder- ½ teaspoon

Onion powder- ½ teaspoon

Garlic powder- 1 teaspoon

Smoked paprika- ½ teaspoon

Cumin- ¼ teaspoon

Sea salt- ½ teaspoon

Black pepper- ¼ teaspoon

Water/Broth- 1 cup

BBQ sauce

NUTRITION INFORMATION:

Total fat: 9 g

Carbohydrate: 2 g

Fiber: 1 g

Sugar: 1 g

Protein: 21 g

DIRECTIONS:

1. To prepare the spice rub, combine chili powder, onion powder, garlic powder, smoked paprika, cumin, black pepper and sea salt in a bowl.

2. Cut the ribs into 3 even portions and rub the spice mixture in each section.

3. In the bottom of the Instant Pot, place a metal rack. Add broth or water.

4. Arrange the spice-rubbed baby ribs on the metal rack.

5. Lock the lid and press the manual function to cook the ribs for 30 minutes.

6. Vent the pot and quick release the steam.

7. Remove the ribs and keep them aside. Preheat the broiler at medium-high heat. Brush the ribs using barbecue sauce on each side.

8. Broil the ribs for 3-5 minutes until caramelized.

9. Cut the ribs into bite-size pieces and serve.

PULLED PORK IN BBQ SAUCE

SERVING SIZE: 1 PORTION
SERVINGS PER RECIPE: 8
CALORIES: 417 PER SERVING
PREPARATION TIME: 5 MINUTES
COOKING TIME: 1 HOUR 30 MINUTES

INGREDIENTS:

- Pork shoulder- 4 lbs., bone in
- Garlic powder- 1 tablespoon
- Onion powder- 1 tablespoon
- Smoked paprika- 1 tablespoon
- Chili powder- 1 tablespoon
- Chicken stock- 2 cups
- Ground pepper- 1 tablespoon
- Sea salt- 1 tablespoon
- Tomato paste- ¼ cup
- Dates- 4 to 6, soaked
- Coconut aminos- ½ cup

NUTRITION INFORMATION:

- Total fat: 11 g
- Carbohydrate: 47 g
- Fiber: 3 g
- Sugar: 38 g
- Protein: 33 g

DIRECTIONS:

1. In a small bowl, add all the seasonings and spices. Mix well to prepare a spice rub.

2. Cut the roast into two portions and coat it with spice rub.

3. Place the marinated pork in the bottom of the Instant Pot with skin side up. Pour in the chicken stock. On the manual setting, cook for next 90 minutes.

4. Meanwhile, prepare your BBQ sauce. Add all the ingredients for the sauce in the food processor and blend everything well. Blend until it smoothens down and forms the consistency of a sauce. Store it in the fridge.

5. Allow the pressure to release manually for next 10-15 minutes and do not choose the quick release function.

6. Remove the pork from the pot and shred it before serving. Pour the sauce over the shredded pork and mix.

7. Serve the spicy pork in BBQ sauce!

PINEAPPLE PORK STEW

SERVING SIZE: 1 CUP
SERVINGS PER RECIPE: 6
CALORIES: 225 PER SERVING
PREPARATION TIME: 10 MINUTES
COOKING TIME: 45 MINUTES

INGREDIENTS:

- Pork- 2 lbs., cubed
- Pineapple- 1 cup, cubed
- Ground cloves- ½ teaspoon
- Sea salt- ½ teaspoon
- Coconut aminos- 1 tablespoon
- Turmeric powder- ½ teaspoon
- Ginger powder- ½ teaspoon
- Onion- 1, large size, sliced
- Ground cinnamon- 1 teaspoon
- Garlic cloves- 2, large size, chopped
- Bay leaf- 1
- Bone broth- 1 cup
- Dates- 2 tablespoon, chopped
- Swiss chard- 1 bunch

NUTRITION INFORMATION:

- Total fat: 6 g
- Carbohydrate: 0 g
- Fiber: 3 g
- Sugar: 0 g
- Protein: 24 g

DIRECTIONS:

1. Take a bowl and prepare a dry marinade for the pork. Combine sea salt, coconut aminos, cassava flour, ginger powder, ground cloves and turmeric powder and marinate the pork cubes with it. Keep the marinated pork aside for 1 hour before cooking.

2. Use the sauté setting to heat the pot. Add oil and onions and sauté it for a minute, and then add garlic until mixed well. Remove the mixture and keep it aside.

3. Add the pork cubes to the pot and cook them until brown.

4. Remove the pork from the pot and add broth. Now, transfer the onion & garlic mixture and pork cubes again in the pot. Add in pineapple chunks, cinnamon, chard stems, jam and bay leaf to the pot.

5. Seal the pot and press the stew/meat function. Cook for 35 minutes.

6. As soon as the timer beeps, quick release the pressure using the vent functions.

7. Set the pot to the sauté setting again and add the Swiss chard leaves to it.

8. Simmer the contents until the leaves are cooked and gravy gets gravy-like consistency. Remove the bay leaf.

9. Season the pineapple pork stew with salt and pepper as per taste and serve.

GREEN CHILI PORK

SERVING SIZE: 1 SERVING
SERVINGS PER RECIPE: 8
CALORIES: 140 PER SERVING
PREPARATION TIME: 30 MINUTES
COOKING TIME: 35 MINUTES

INGREDIENTS:

- Pork shoulder- 3 pounds, roast, sliced
- Garlic powder- 2 teaspoons
- Cumin- 2 teaspoons
- Tapioca- 2 tablespoons
- Coriander- 1 teaspoon
- Sea salt- 1 teaspoon
- Coconut oil- 3 tablespoons
- Juice of ½ lime
- Broth

NUTRITION INFORMATION:

- Total fat: 5 g
- Carbohydrate: 11 g
- Fiber: 1 g
- Sugar: 0 g
- Protein: 12 g

DIRECTIONS:

1. Preheat the Instant Pot at sautéing setting while preparing for the taco filling.

2. In a bowl, mix all the spices and herbs. Use this to coat the pork slices evenly.

3. Place the slices on the bottom of the pot and cook until brown. Toss after 3-5 minutes to cook on another side.

4. Add lime juice once the pork is done and lock the lid. Select the stew/meat setting and cook the contents for 35 minutes at high pressure.

5. Select cancel and quick release after 15 minutes.

6. To boil and simmer the pork, hit the sauté setting again.

7. Your pork filling is ready to be served with tacos!

BALSAMIC PORK TENDERLOIN

SERVING SIZE: 1 SERVING
SERVINGS PER RECIPE: 8
CALORIES: 228 PER SERVING
PREPARATION TIME: 5 MINUTES
COOKING TIME: 20 MINUTES

INGREDIENTS:

- Pork tenderloin- 1.5 lbs.
- Chicken broth- 1/3 cup
- Balsamic vinegar- 1/3 cup
- Olive oil- 2 teaspoons
- Honey- 1 tablespoon
- Salt and pepper- as per taste
- Baby carrots- 2 cups
- Red potatoes- 2 cups, cubed

NUTRITION INFORMATION:

- Total fat: 10 g
- Carbohydrate: 1 g
- Fiber: 0 g
- Sugar: 1 g
- Protein: 31 g

DIRECTIONS:

1. Select the sauté function on your Instant Pot and let it heat up. Once it displays hot, add olive oil to the bottom of the pot. Sauté the pork tenderloin on all the sides until brown. Season the pork with pepper and salt. You can add potatoes and carrots to the pot on top of pork.

2. Mix honey, broth and balsamic together and pour this mixture over the veggies and pork. Lock the Instant Pot and cook for minutes at high pressure. Release the pressure for 6 minutes using quick release.

3. Transfer the pork from the pot to the serving plate and allow it to rest. Meanwhile, prepare the gravy in Instant Pot. Switch to sauté and add a small amount of thickener. Keep stirring to form gravy and season as per taste.

4. Pour gravy over the pork before serving and slice.

PORK RAGU

SERVING SIZE: 1 SERVING
SERVINGS PER RECIPE: 5
CALORIES: 406 PER SERVING
PREPARATION TIME: 10 MINUTES
COOKING TIME: 25 MINUTES

INGREDIENTS:

- Pork shoulder- 1 lb.
- Noodles- 12 oz.
- Garlic cloves- 5
- Onion- 1, chopped
- Tomatoes- 14 oz.
- Tomato paste- 1 tablespoon
- Broth- 1 cup
- Oregano- 1 teaspoon, dried
- Red wine- ½ cup, dry
- Olive oil- 1 tablespoon

NUTRITION INFORMATION:

- Total fat: 19 g
- Carbohydrate: 15 g
- Fiber: 0 g
- Sugar: 11 g
- Protein: 31 g

DIRECTIONS:

1. Select the sauté settings on the Instant Pot. Heat the olive oil in it, and smoke onions and pork it. Sauté for next 5 minutes until the pork turns brown.
2. Add garlic to the pot and cook for another 1 minute, stirring occasionally. Add tomatoes, broth, red dry wine, tomatoes and dried oregano.
3. Press the off button and seal button. Select the stew settings and cook the contents for 25 minutes at high pressure. Quick release the pressure and shred the chicken in the pot itself, stirring well.
4. Cook noodles and serve pork ragu on top of it. Enjoy!

TERIYAKI PORK TENDERLOIN

SERVING SIZE: 4 OZ
SERVINGS PER RECIPE: 4
CALORIES: 220 PER SERVING
PREPARATION TIME: 5 MINUTES
COOKING TIME: 12 MINUTES

INGREDIENTS:

- Pork tenderloin- 21 Oz
- Coconut aminos- 1/3 cup
- Garlic cloves- 2, crushed
- Water- ½ cup
- Ground ginger- 1 teaspoon
- Brown sugar- 2 tablespoons
- Onion powder- ½ teaspoon
- Rice vinegar- 1 teaspoon
- Sesame oil- 1 teaspoon
- Spring onion- 2, chopped
- Arrowroot powder- 1 tablespoon
- Sesame seeds
- Black pepper and salt as per taste

NUTRITION INFORMATION:

- Total fat: 6.2 g
- Carbohydrate: 8.4 g
- Fiber: 0.3 g
- Sugar: 4.5 g
- Protein: 32.7 g

DIRECTIONS:

1. Place the pork tenderloin in the Instant Pot.

2. Take a bowl and add vinegar, soy sauce, water, ginger, garlic, brown sugar, and onion powder and sesame oil. Whisk everything together.

3. Pour this freshly prepared mixture in the Instant Pot over the pork tenderloin.

4. Toss the pork tenderloin in the pot so it gets evenly coated in the sauce. Cook it at high pressure for next 5 minutes. Close the valve.

5. Allow the pressure to release for additional 7 minutes. Remove the pork from the Instant Pot and place it in the serving dish, covered with foil. Leave the sauce in the Instant Pot only.

6. Set the Instant Pot to sauté mode. Add arrowroot powder and water to prepare gravy. Stir until the sauce thickens.

7. Shred the pork or slice it and add to the sauce on the pot. Season with salt and pepper as per taste.

8. Sprinkle the pork with chopped spring onions and sesame seeds. Serve hot.

SMOKY CHILI BACON

SERVING SIZE: 4 OUNCES
SERVINGS PER RECIPE: 4
CALORIES: 342 PER SERVING
PREPARATION TIME: 15 MINUTES
COOKING TIME: 50 MINUTES

INGREDIENTS:

- Bacon- 6 sliced
- Onion- 1, diced
- Garlic cloves- 2, minced
- Green bell pepper- 1, diced
- Red bell pepper- 1, diced
- Paprika- 1 tablespoon
- Chili powder- 1 tablespoon
- Garlic powder- 1 tablespoon
- Cayenne pepper- ½ teaspoon
- Cumin- 2 teaspoons
- Fire roasted tomatoes- 14 ounce
- Tomato sauce- 8 ounce
- Coconut cream- ½ cup
- Ranch dressing- 2 tablespoons
- Cilantro
- Salt and pepper- as per taste

NUTRITION INFORMATION:

- Total fat: 19 g
- Carbohydrate: 18 g
- Fiber: 0 g
- Sugar: 0 g
- Protein: 25 g

DIRECTIONS:

1. Place the bacon slices in the pot brushed with oil. Select the sauté option and cook until the bacon becomes crispy.

2. Once the bacon is done, transfer it to a plate and add onion, garlic cloves, and pepper to the pot and sauté it in the bacon fat for next 5 minutes.

3. Add the leftover ingredients to the pot and combine everything well. Once the contents are brought to boil for 5 more minutes, add the bacon back to the pot and mix well with the sauce. Select the keep warm setting and secure the lid.

4. Now, close the valve and select the chili or bean function. Cook the meat for 30 minutes. You can either release the pressure naturally or use quick release. Stir well.

5. Mix ranch dressing and coconut cream together to prepare a dressing for the dish.

6. Plop it over the pork and garnish with cilantro. Serve.

SAUSAGE AND SHRIMP GUMBO

SERVING SIZE: 1 CUP
SERVINGS PER RECIPE: 4
CALORIES: 296 PER SERVING
PREPARATION TIME: 5 MINUTES
COOKING TIME: 25 MINUTES

INGREDIENTS:

- Pork Sausage- 12 ounces
- Shrimp- 1 pound
- Olive oil- 2 tablespoons
- Celery ribs- 2, diced
- Red bell pepper- 1, diced
- Yellow onion- 1, diced
- Tomatoes- 14.5 ounces, diced
- Cajun seasoning- 2 tablespoons
- Chicken stock- 2/3 cup
- Bay leaves- 2
- Black pepper
- Salt
- Parsley/Chives- for garnishing

NUTRITION INFORMATION:

- Total fat: 18 g
- Carbohydrate: 21 g
- Fiber: 2 g
- Sugar: 3 g
- Protein: 21 g

DIRECTIONS:

1. Add olive oil to the bottom of the pot. Select the sauté function. When the pot becomes hot, add sausage to it and cook until it turns brown. Sear on each side for 2-3 minutes. Transfer the sausage to the plate using a slotted spoon.

2. Now, add celery, pepper, Cajun seasoning and onion to the pot. Sauté the contents for next 1-2 minutes until the mixture becomes fragrant. Add the sausage again to the pot along with chicken stock, tomatoes and bay leaves. Stir everything well.

3. Secure the lid of the Instant Pot and set it to the sealing position. Choose the manual option and set the timer for 5 minutes. Let the contents cook at high pressure.

4. As soon as the timer beeps, press the cancel function. Choose the venting position to release the steam manually. Remove the lid from the pot and press the sauté function again. Add shrimp to the pot and cook for next 3-4 minutes. Make sure the shrimps turn opaque. Season the gumbo with sea salt and ground pepper.

5. Serve the freshly prepared gumbo, garnished with chives and parsley.

KALUA PORK

SERVING SIZE: 1 SERVING
SERVINGS PER RECIPE: 8
CALORIES: 415 PER SERVING
PREPARATION TIME: 15 MINUTES
COOKING TIME: 90 MINUTES

INGREDIENTS:

Pork shoulder roast- 5 pounds, bone in

Bacon slices- 3

Garlic cloves- 5

Water- 1 cup

Hawaiian sea salt- 1 ½ tablespoons

Cabbage- 1, chopped

NUTRITION INFORMATION:

Total fat: 30 g

Carbohydrate: 5 g

Fiber: 2 g

Sugar: 0 g

Protein: 30 g

DIRECTIONS:

1. Add the slices of bacon to the bottom of the pot. Use the sauté setting to cook the bacon. Keep on cooking until the bacon starts to sizzle up and turns brown on each side evenly. Turn off the settings.

2. In a separate dish, season the pork using garlic cloves and salt. Once the pork has been seasoned properly, place this in the instant pot over the cooked slices of bacon.

3. Pour in about 1 cup of water and lock the lid.

4. Press the manual button and set the timer to about 90 minutes. Make sure the pressure settings are on high. Once the Instant Pot is programmed, keep it aside and wait for the timer to beep.

5. Once the stew is cooked, press the keep warm button. This will turn off the pot. Now wait for the steam to release naturally. Shred the pork in the pot itself.

6. Transfer the shredded pork to serving dish. Pour in the extra cooking liquid. Season the pork with salt and pepper as per taste desired.

7. Now, chop the cabbage and cook it under high pressure for next 3-5 minutes in the same pot. Release the pressure using the quick release mode once the cabbage is cooked. If you want the main dish to have a stew like consistency, cook the cabbage in the same cooking liquid in which the pork was cooked.

8. Pour the leftover liquid over the shredded pork. Garnish the Hawaiian Style Kalua pork with steamed cabbage. Serve hot.

INSTANT POT WHOLE 30 BEEF RECIPES

BEEF, BROCCOLI AND ZUCCHINI SOUP

SERVING SIZE: 1 CUP
SERVINGS PER RECIPE: 6
CALORIES: 159 PER SERVING
PREPARATION TIME: 10 MINUTES
COOKING TIME: 15 MINUTES

INGREDIENTS:

- Steak tips- 1.5 lbs.
- Avocado oil- 2 tablespoons
- Garlic cloves- 2, minced
- Ginger- 3 tablespoons, minced
- Mushrooms- 8 oz., sliced
- Broccoli florets- 2 cups
- Broth- 6 cups
- Coconut aminos- ½ cup
- Apple cider vinegar- ¼ cup
- Sriracha- ¼ cup
- Zucchini- 1, large size, spiraled
- Green onion- 1/3 cup, chopped

NUTRITION INFORMATION:

- Total fat: 5 g
- Carbohydrate: 11 g
- Fiber: 3 g
- Sugar: 0 g
- Protein: 18 g

DIRECTIONS:

1. Heat the pot on sauté mode and add ginger, avocado oil, steak tips and garlic to it once hot. Cook for few minutes until the beef turns brown and ginger and garlic becomes fragrant. Select the cancel mode.

2. Now add mushrooms, broccoli, vinegar, beef broth, Sriracha and coconut aminos. Stir well and seal the pot's lid.

3. Cook on the high pressure at manual settings for 8 minutes. Quick release to remove the steam.

4. Unlock the lid; add more sauce as per the level of spiciness required. Add zucchini, garnish with green onions and serve hot.

MEXICAN STYLE BEEF

SERVING SIZE: 1 SERVING
SERVINGS PER RECIPE: 6
CALORIES: 219 PER SERVING
PREPARATION TIME: 5 MINUTES
COOKING TIME: 35 MINUTES

INGREDIENTS:

- Beef short ribs or beef brisket- 2 ½ pounds, boneless
- Onion- 1, medium size, sliced
- Garlic cloves- 6, peeled
- Tomato salsa- ½ cup
- Tomato paste- 1 tablespoon
- Chili powder- 1 tablespoon
- Ghee- 1 tablespoon
- Broth- ½ cup
- Fish sauce- ½ teaspoon
- Radish- 2, sliced
- Cilantro- ½ cup, minced
- Kosher salt- 1 ½ teaspoons
- Black pepper

NUTRITION INFORMATION:

- Total fat: 11 g
- Carbohydrate: 1 g
- Fiber: 0 g
- Sugar: 1 g
- Protein: 27 g

DIRECTIONS:

1. Take a large bowl and add chili powder and salt to it. Season the beef cubes with it.

2. Add ghee to the pot and press the sauté setting for the ghee to melt. Once hot, sauté the onions in it until they turn translucent.

3. Pour in garlic and tomato paste and cook for additional 30 seconds until the mixture becomes fragrant.

4. Add the seasoned beef cubes to the pot and pour fish sauce, broth, and salsa on top of it.

5. Cover the pot with help of a lid and cook at manual settings.

6. Make sure the beef is well cooked under high pressure at the end of 35 minutes. Do not choose the quick release option; instead, allow the steam to release naturally in 15 minutes.

7. Unlock the lid. Season the beef with salt and pepper as per taste.

8. Serve the hot stew garnished with freshly chopped radishes and cilantro.

PLANTAIN BEEF CURRY

SERVING SIZE: 4.5 OUNCES
SERVINGS PER RECIPE: 5-6
CALORIES: 248 PER SERVING
PREPARATION TIME: 10 MINUTES
COOKING TIME: 30 MINUTES

INGREDIENTS:

- Pot roast- 2 lbs.
- Ripe plantain- 1, sliced
- Coconut oil- 3 teaspoons
- Onions- 2, small size, peeled and sliced
- Coconut oil- 1 cup
- Garlic powder- 1 teaspoon
- Turmeric powder- 1 teaspoon
- Ginger powder- 1 teaspoon
- Sea salt- 1 teaspoon
- Kaffir lime leaves- 4
- Cinnamon- 1 stick
- Coriander leaves- 1 tablespoon, chopped

NUTRITION INFORMATION:

- Total fat: 14 g
- Carbohydrate: 12 g
- Fiber: 1 g
- Sugar: 5 g
- Protein: 19 g

DIRECTIONS:

1. In a separate small bowl, mix ginger powder, garlic powder, sea salt and turmeric powder along with 2 teaspoons of coconut oil. Use this mixture to marinate the beef and allow it to rest for next 1 hour.

2. Set the settings of the Instant Pot to sauté and cook onions in it with coconut oil until the onions turn translucent. Remove the sautéed onions from the pot.

3. Add the marinated beef to the pot and cook until it turns brown. Set it aside.

4. Pour coconut milk into the pot and stir gently along with the browned meat. Add the sautéed onions to it along with cinnamon stick and kaffir lime leaves.

5. Cover the Instant Pot with lid and seal it. Cook the contents on the manual setting for next 35 minutes.

6. As soon as the timer beeps, select cancel and release the pressure naturally.

7. Select the sauté option again and add plantain to the pot. Stir in the sea salt and let it simmer for next 5 minutes until the plantain is cooked and the curry thickens a bit.

8. Remove the kaffir lime leaves and cinnamon stick from the curry before serving. Garnish with chopped coriander and serve.

PLANTAIN BEEF CURRY

SERVING SIZE: 3 OZ
SERVINGS PER RECIPE: 4
CALORIES: 438 PER SERVING
PREPARATION TIME: 10 MINUTES
COOKING TIME: 50 MINUTES

INGREDIENTS:

For the roast:

- Beef roast- 2 pounds
- Beef broth- 1 cup
- Onion- 1, small size, chopped
- Balsamic vinegar- 3 tablespoons
- Figs- 6, dried, chopped
- Brewed coffee- 1 cup
- Black pepper
- Kosher salt

For the mocha rub:

- Paprika- 2 tablespoons
- Cocoa powder- 1 tablespoon
- Ground coffee- 2 tablespoons
- Black pepper- 1 tablespoon
- Chili powder- 1 teaspoon
- Aleppo pepper- 1 teaspoon
- Sea salt- 1 teaspoon
- Ground ginger- 1 teaspoon

NUTRITION INFORMATION:

- Total fat: 23 g
- Carbohydrate: 10 g
- Fiber: 0 g
- Sugar: 0 g
- Protein: 43 g

DIRECTIONS:

1. Take a separate bowl and mix all the ingredients required for the mocha rub in it. Store it aside for further use.

2. In another bowl, add beef cubes and freshly prepared mocha rub. Toss well until each beef cube is evenly coated on each side.

3. In a blender, pour 1 cup brewed coffee, figs, balsamic vinegar, onion, and broth. Blend until sauce-like liquid is received.

4. Add the seasoned beef to the Instant Pot and pour the freshly prepared sauce on top of it.

5. Cover the lid and lock it in the sealing position. Choose the stew/meat option and cook for next 35 minutes. Let the beef cook along with the sauce.

6. When the stew is finished cooking, turn the Instant Pot. Release the pressure naturally for next 15 minutes.

7. Open the lid and shred the meat using a fork. Transfer the cooked beef to the serving dish.

8. Boil the leftover sauce and thicken it. Pour this boiled sauce over the beef and season it with salt and pepper as per taste.

9. Pour the sauce over the beef before serving. Serve hot.

INSTANT ITALIAN BEEF

SERVING SIZE: 1 SERVING
SERVINGS PER RECIPE: 4
CALORIES: 451 PER SERVING
PREPARATION TIME: 10 MINUTES
COOKING TIME: 1 HOUR 10 MINUTES

INGREDIENTS:

- Beef roast- 3 pounds, boneless
- Onion powder- 1 tablespoon
- Garlic powder- 1 tablespoon
- Italian seasoning- 1 tablespoon
- Beef stock- 1 cup
- Fish sauce- 1 tablespoon
- Onion- 1, medium size, sliced
- Olive oil- 2 tablespoons
- Salt and pepper- as per taste

NUTRITION INFORMATION:

- Total fat: 28 g
- Carbohydrate: 60 g
- Fiber: 0 g
- Sugar: 0 g
- Protein: 47 g

DIRECTIONS:

1. Cut the beef chuck into even pieces. Season the beef with pepper, salt, garlic powder, Italian seasoning and onion powder.

2. Turn the sauté setting on. Once the pot becomes hot, add olive oil to it to coat the bottom of the pot. Add meat to the pot and sear it.

3. Sear the meat in the pot until it turns brown from all sides. As soon as the meat gets done, pour the beef stock in it along with fish sauce. Press the cancel button and scrap the bottom of the cooked meat.

4. Place a trivet in the liner and add onion slices and sautéed meat in it.

5. Lock the Instant Pot and seal it. The valve must be at the sealing position. Select the manual or meat setting and set the timer for 60 minutes.

6. Meanwhile, the meat cooks, slice the bell peppers and coat it with a mixture of pepper, salt, and garlic powder. Heat a skillet and sauté the coated pepper slices in it with olive oil. Make sure the bell peppers become soft.

7. Once the cooker beeps, release the steam naturally for next 15 minutes. Open the valve to let out the remaining pressure.

8. Shred the beef in the pot and mix it with softened bell peppers.

9. Serve hot with mashed potatoes, Italian roll or green salad.

BEEF BARBACOA

SERVING SIZE: 1 CUP
SERVINGS PER RECIPE: 8
CALORIES: 230 PER SERVING
PREPARATION TIME: 5 MINUTES
COOKING TIME: 90 MINUTES

INGREDIENTS:

- Beef roast- 4 lbs., boneless
- Avocado oil- 2 tablespoons
- Beef broth- 1.5 cups
- Onion- 1, small size, sliced
- Apple cider vinegar- 3 tablespoons
- Tomato paste- 2 tablespoons
- Ground cumin- 1 teaspoon
- Chipotle chili powder- 1 tablespoon
- Garlic cloves- 4, minced
- Oregano- 1 teaspoon
- Bay leaf- 2
- Kosher salt

NUTRITION INFORMATION:

- Total fat: 19 g
- Carbohydrate – 1 g
- Fiber: 0 g
- Sugar: 0 g
- Protein: 14 g

DIRECTIONS:

1. Cut the beef chuck into 5-6 portions of meat. Season well with kosher salt.

2. Select the sauté button on Instant Pot and add oil to the bottom of the pot. Sear the meat in the pot until it turns brown on all sides. Make sure the meat is seared on each side for 3 minutes. Set it aside on a plate once done.

3. Once the beef is removed, add onions to the bottom of the pot along with oil. Heat and sauté the onions for next 4 minutes.

4. Select the cancel mode on the Instant Pot. Add the meat back to the pot and toss it with the onions.

5. Take a separate bowl and mix tomato paste, apple cider vinegar, beef broth, cumin, chipotle powder, garlic and oregano in it. Whisk the ingredients until everything well combined.

6. Pour the freshly prepared sauce over the meat in the Instant Pot. Add the bay leaves and cover the lid. Lock it the place and select the manual settings to cook for next 90 minutes under pressure.

7. As soon as the timer beeps, switch the Instant Pot to the keep warm mode.

8. Release the pressure automatically using the quick release option. Once the venting process is over, transfer the meat to the cooking sheet. Shred it using forks or tongs.

9. Mix the shredded meat with the sauce properly before serving.

10. Drain the excess sauce and then serve.

THAI BEEF LETTUCE WRAPS

SERVING SIZE: 1 PLATE
SERVINGS PER RECIPE: 6-8
CALORIES: 611 PER SERVING
PREPARATION TIME: 15 MINUTES
COOKING TIME: 20 MINUTES

INGREDIENTS:
- Beefsteak- 2 lbs., sliced
- Avocado oil- 2 tablespoons
- Ginger- 3 tablespoons, chopped
- White onion- 1 cup, diced
- Garlic- 1 tablespoon, minced
- Tomatoes- ½ cup, diced
- Red bell pepper- 1, large, diced
- Juice of ½ lime
- Water- ½ cup
- Thai curry paste- ½ cup
- Beef broth- 2 cups
- Coconut milk- ½ cup
- Arrowroot starch- 3 tablespoons
- Lettuce
- Salt- as per taste
- Carrots- 1 cup, shredded
- Purple cabbage- 1/3 cup
- Cilantro- 1/3 cup

NUTRITION INFORMATION:
- Total fat: 40 g
- Carbohydrates: 25 g
- Fiber: 5 g
- Sugar: 0 g
- Protein: 37 g

DIRECTIONS:

1. Select the sauté function on your Instant Pot and let it heat up. Add oil and toss onion in it once the pot gets hot. Sauté the onion for 2-3 minutes and then add beef to the pot. Cook the beef until it turns brown from each side.

2. In the pot, add ginger, garlic, lime juice, bell pepper, curry paste, water, broth and tomatoes on top of the beef. Secure the lid properly.

3. Cancel the sauté process and select the manual function at high pressure. Set the timer for 11 minutes. Let everything cook

4. Release the steam naturally. It will take about 15 minutes.

5. Remove the lid, mix coconut milk and arrowroot starch in the pot. Let the contents settle for a bit. Prepare the lettuce wraps meanwhile and season the beef mixture with salt.

6. Add the beef mixture to the lettuce wrap garnished with lime juice, carrots, and cilantro.

7. Serve and enjoy the delicious taste of Thai beef lettuce wraps.

ABOUT THE AUTHOR

James Houck is a health and fitness enthusiast who loves teaching people about healthy ways to lose weight and live the best life they can.

Over the years, he has studied what works and what doesn't in health and fitness. He is passionate about helping others achieve great success in their diet and exercise endeavor through his books and seminars.

His biggest satisfaction is when he finds out that he was able to help someone attain the results they've been looking for. In his free time, he loves to spend time with his 2-year-old daughter.

Made in the USA
Middletown, DE
17 July 2018